001 002 003

G. Sturm: Decorative Application of the Colors of a Butterfly

300 ART NOUVEAU DESIGNS AND MOTIFS IN FULL COLOR

Edited by
CAROL BELANGER GRAFTON

DOVER PUBLICATIONS, INC., NEW YORK

Publisher's Note

In 1890, the Stuttgart publishing house of Julius Hoffmann brought out the first issue of *Dekorative Vorbilder* (Decorative Models/Patterns), described by the press as "a compilation of figurative representations, applied-art embellishments, plastic ornaments, decorative animal and plant studies, allegories, trophies, heraldic motifs, club insignias, coats of arms for guilds, festive ornaments, etc." For the next two and a half decades, the journal's lavishly printed pages displayed hundreds of examples of European Art Nouveau design intended to inspire painters, graphic artists, designers, interior decorators, sculptors and architects.

The 45 plates selected for this book by Carol Belanger Grafton from volumes 8, 10, 11, 13, 15–21 and 23 (1897–1912) are particularly rich in borders, corners, panels large and small, friezes and wall decorations. Forms from nature, especially floral motifs, abound. Oriental influences are evident throughout, as in the fish and dragon panels on plate 13. Some of the more starkly geometric designs, such as those on plates 5, 16 and 21, seem to prefigure the Art Deco movement of later years. Pastel shades dominate the compositions, and the flowing curves so characteristic of Art Nouveau evoke a certain dreaminess.

This addition to Dover's extensive library of Art Nouveau design is published in much the same spirit as the original (and now very rare) *Dekorative Vorbilder,* to provide today's artists and craftspeople with exemplary work of the period, whether for direct, copyright-free use, or for adaptation to a multiplicity of new applications. Connoisseurs of the style will agree that this material is as fresh now as it was nearly one hundred years ago.

300 Art Nouveau Designs and Motifs in Full Color is a new work, first published by Dover Publications, Inc., in 1983.

DOVER *Pictorial Archive* SERIES

This book belongs to the Dover Pictorial Archive Series. You may use the designs and illustrations for graphics and crafts applications, free and without special permission, provided that you include no more than ten in the same publication or project. (For permission for additional use, please write to Dover Publications, Inc., 31 East 2nd Street, Mineola, N.Y. 11501.)

However, republication or reproduction of any illustration by any other graphic service, whether it be in a book or in any other design resource, is strictly prohibited.

Manufactured in the United States of America
Dover Publications, Inc., 31 East 2nd Street, Mineola, N.Y. 11501

Library of Congress Cataloging-in-Publication Data

Main entry under title:

300 art nouveau designs and motifs in full color.

(Dover pictorial archive series)
Selected from Dekorative Vorbilder.
1. Decoration and ornament—Art nouveau.   I. Graton, Carol Belanger.   II. Dekorative Vorbilder.   III. Title: Three hundred art nouveau designs and motifs in full color.   IV. Series.
NK1380.A13   1983   745.4′441   82-9435
ISBN 0-486-24354-0   AACR2

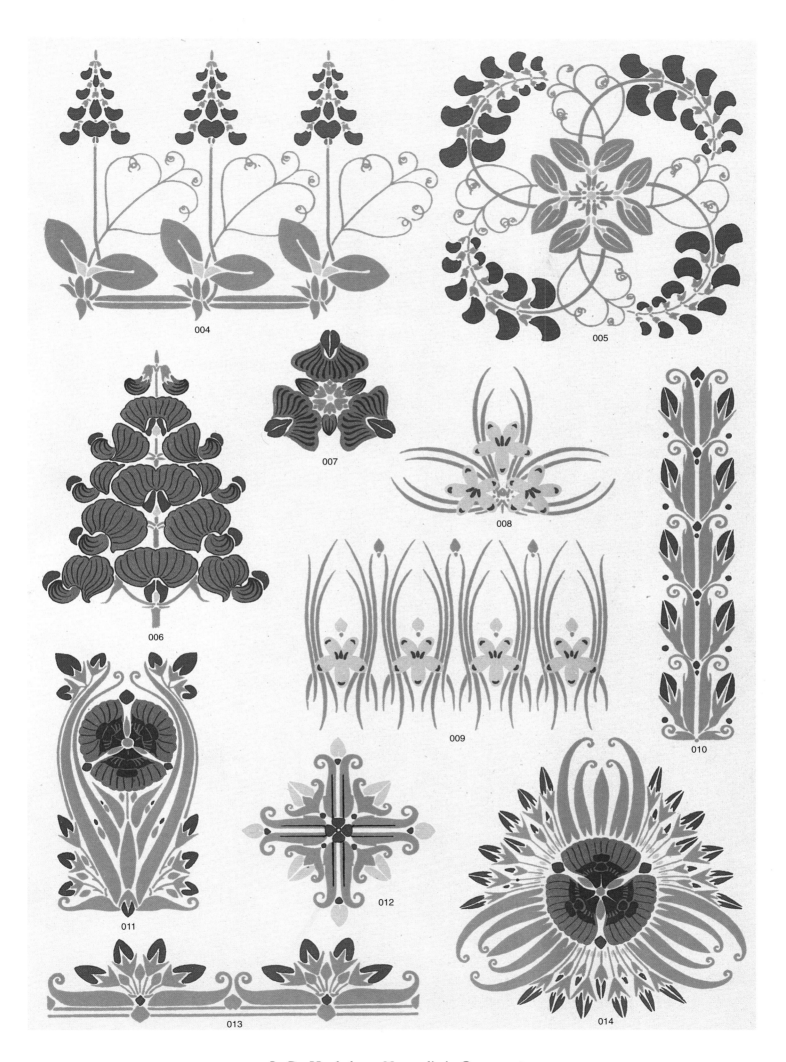

004
005
006
007
008
009
010
011
012
013
014

J. B. Heukelom: Naturalistic Ornament

015

016

017

018

019

020

2

027

028

029

030

031

R. Rochga: Wall Decorations for Stenciling

4

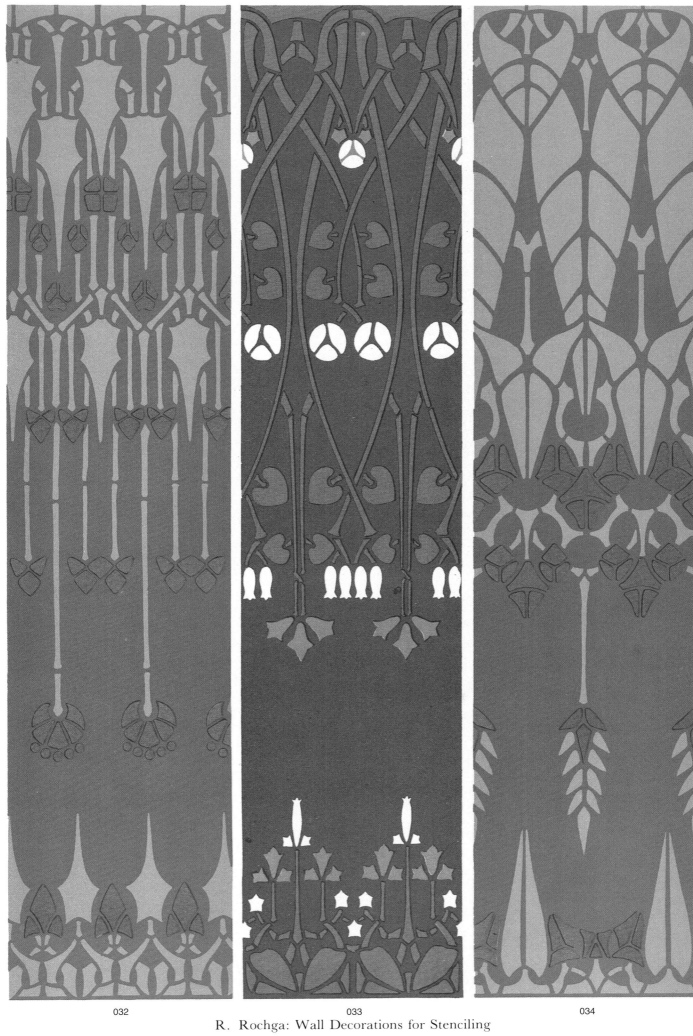

032   033   034

R. Rochga: Wall Decorations for Stenciling

035

036

037

038

039

040

041

R. Godron: Square Panels in Modern Style

042

043

044

045

046

047

048

R. Godron: Square Panels in Modern Style

049

050

051

052

053

054

055

056

057

M. Dufrène: Modern Ornament

058

060

061

062

059

063

064

Anonymous: Ornament

065

066

067

068

069

070

071

072

073

R. Bacard: Floral Ornament

074

075

076

077

078

079

R. Bacard: Floral Panels

080

081

R. Godron: Corners and Borders

082

083

084

085

086

087

088

089

090

091

092

093

R. Godron: Allegories of the Elements and Floral Borders

13

094

095

096

098

097

099

100

H. de Waroquier: Square Panels, Corner and Friezes

14

101

102

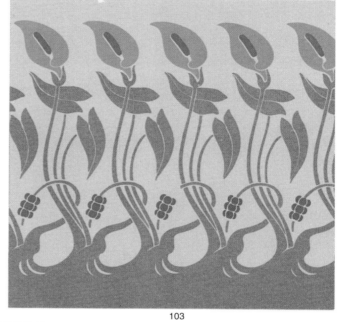

103

104

C. Jacobs: Wall Friezes

15

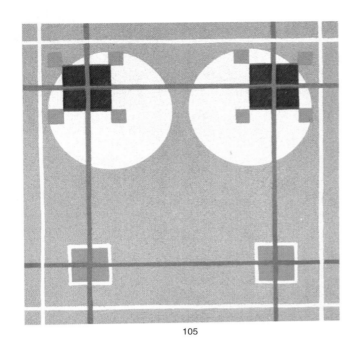

105

106

107

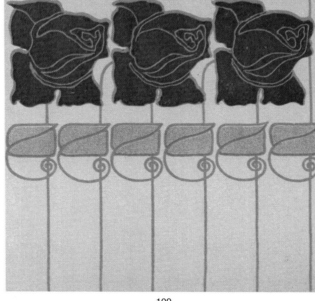

109

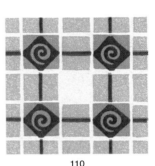

110

111

108

112

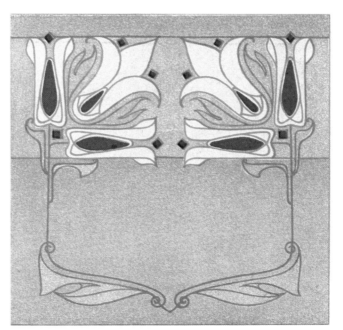

113

R. Beauclair: Square Panels

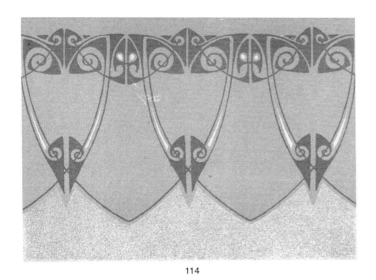

114

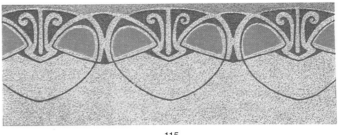

115

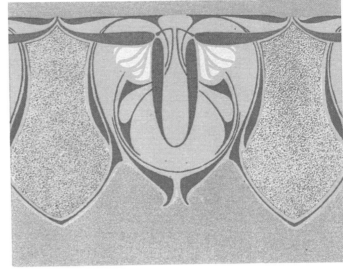

116

117

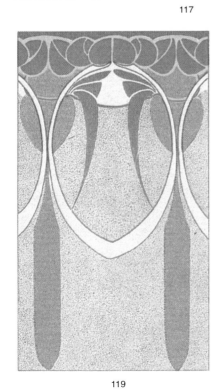

119

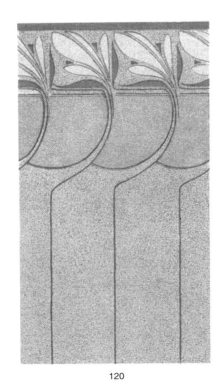

120

121

118

R. Beauclair: Wall Friezes

17

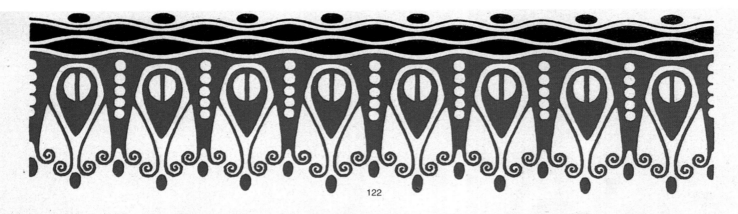

122

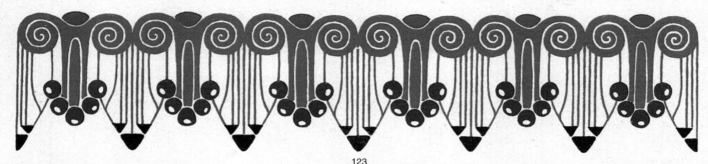

123

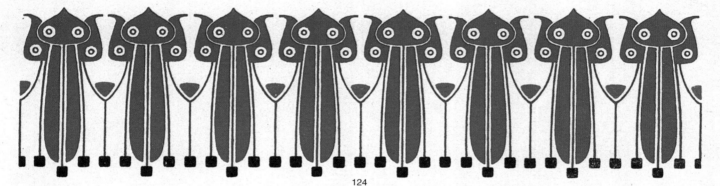

124

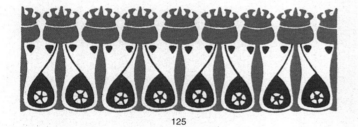

125

126

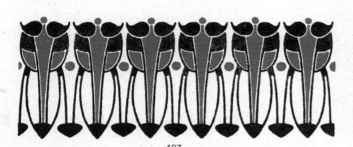

127

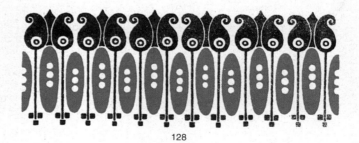

128

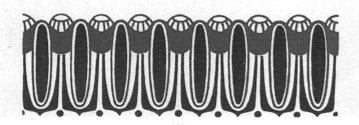

129

130

E. Gradl: Modern Borders

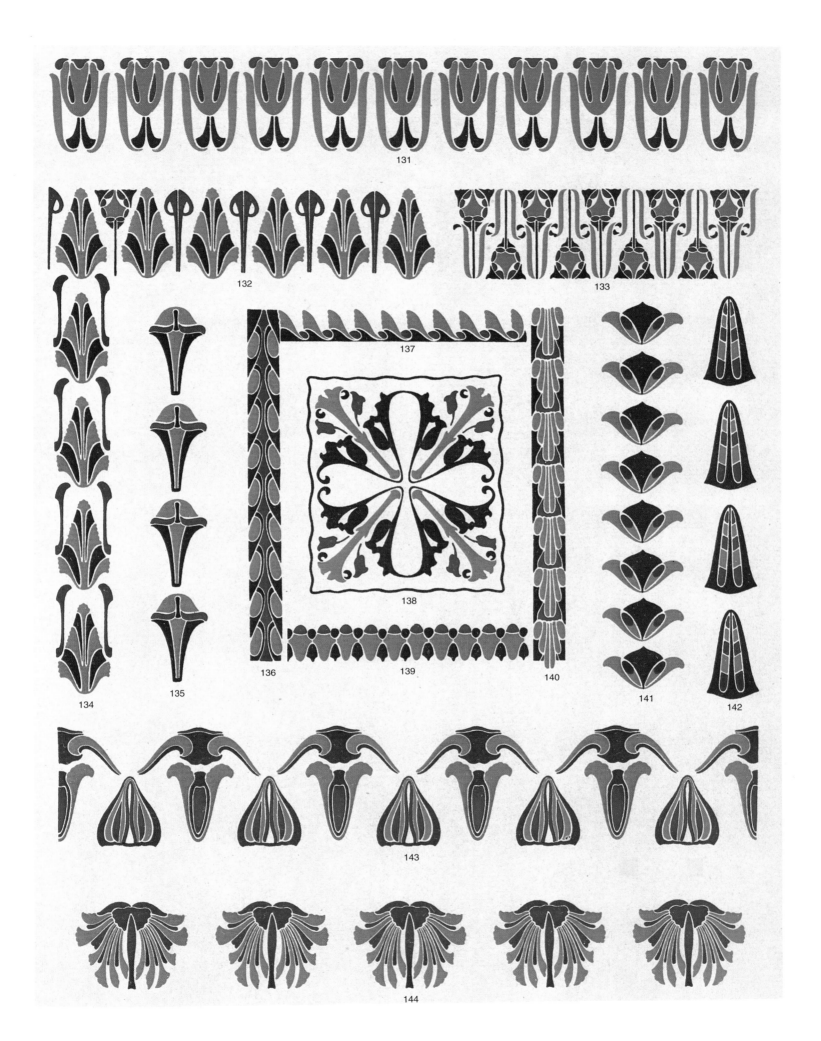

131

132   133

134   135   136   137   138   139   140   141   142

143

144

F. W. Jochem: Modern Friezes

145

146

147

148

149

150

151

152

153

154

L. Popineau: Fish Motifs

157

156

A. Smit: Panels

155

21

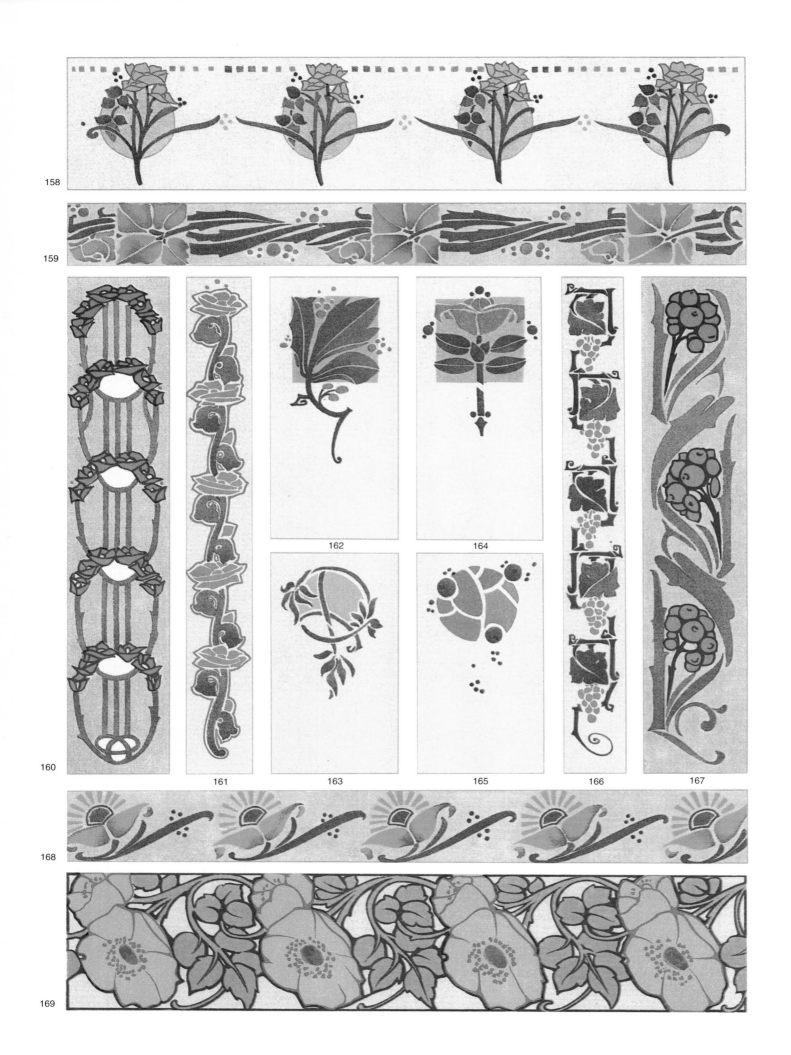

158

159

160

161

162

163

164

165

166

167

168

169

T. Merry: Friezes and Panels

170

171

172

173

Pupils of J. Benes: Stylized Trees

174   175   176   177   178

H. E. Simpson: Pilaster Panels

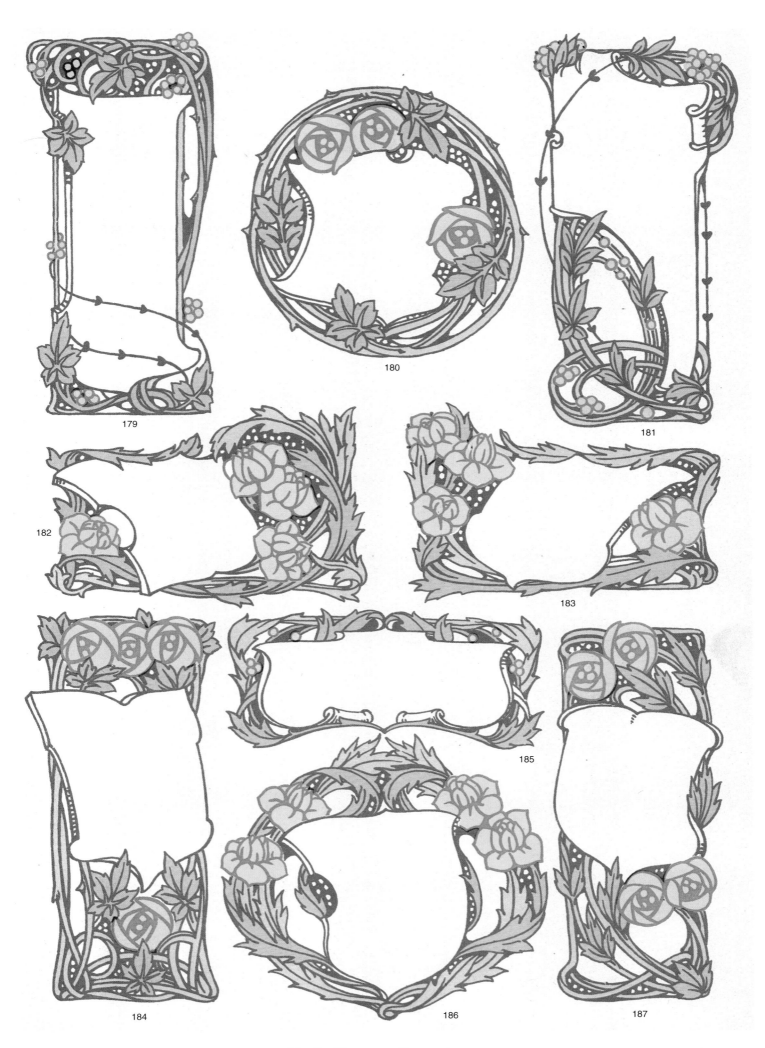

179

180

181

182

183

184

185

186

187

H. E. Simpson: Cartouches

25

188

191

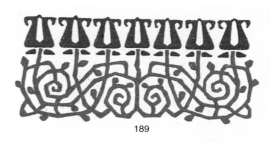

189

190

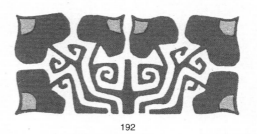

192

193

194

195

196

197

198

199

200

201

202

203

E. Gradl: Small Panels

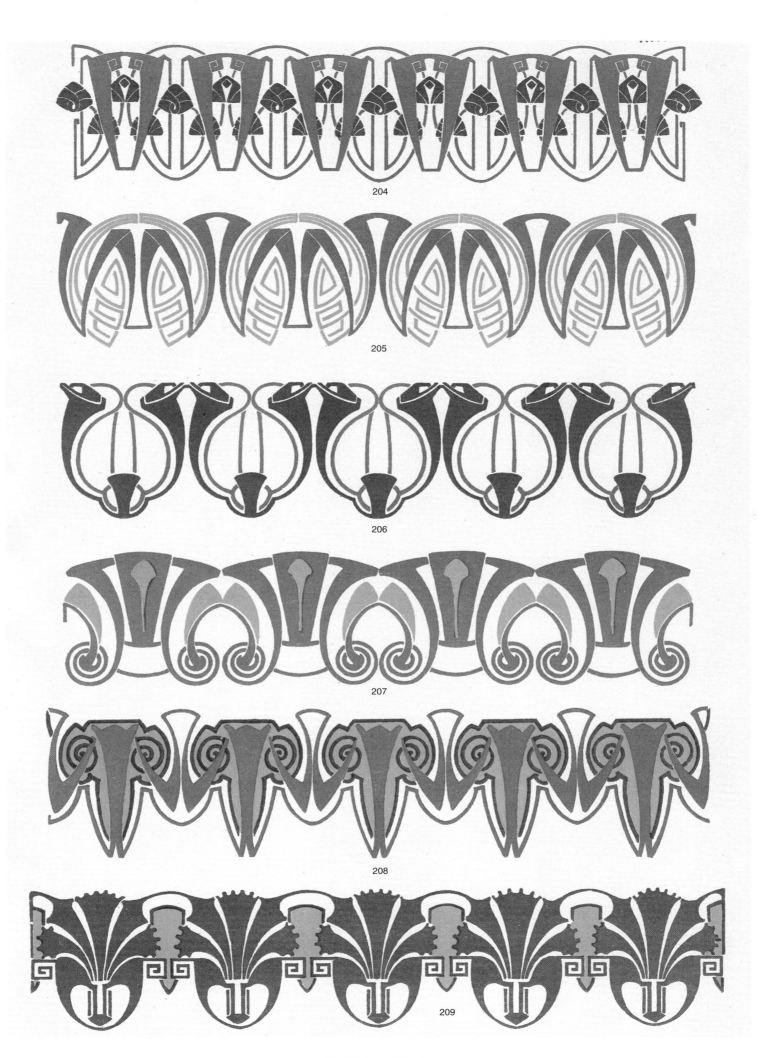

204

205

206

207

208

209

P. Huber: Borders

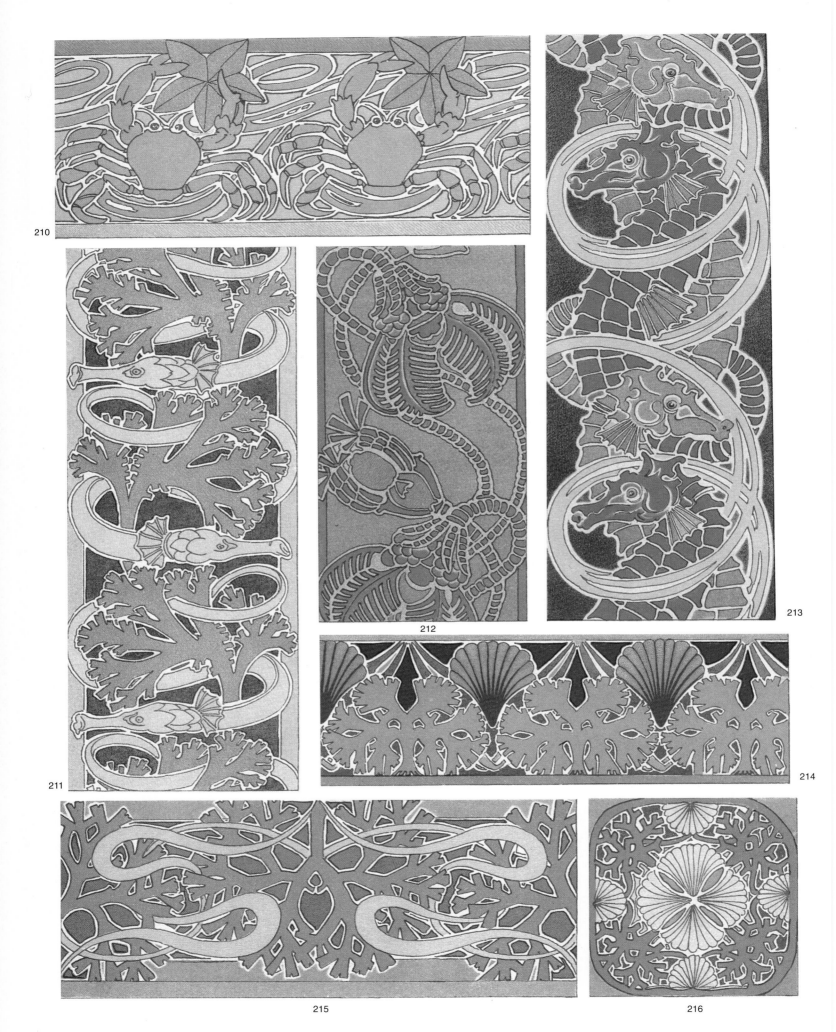

210

211

212

213

214

215

216

L. Popineau: Sea Creatures and Plants

217 218 219 220 221 222 223

L. Popineau: Modern Borders

29

224

225

226

227

228

H. E. von Berlepsch: Window Frames

229

230

H. E. von Berlepsch: Wall Friezes

231

232   233

234   235

236   237

238   239

240   241

242   243

244

R. Godron: Floral Borders

245

246

247

248

249

250

J. Pfeiffer: Floral Borders

251

252

253

254

255

256

C. Martin: Modern Ornaments and Panels

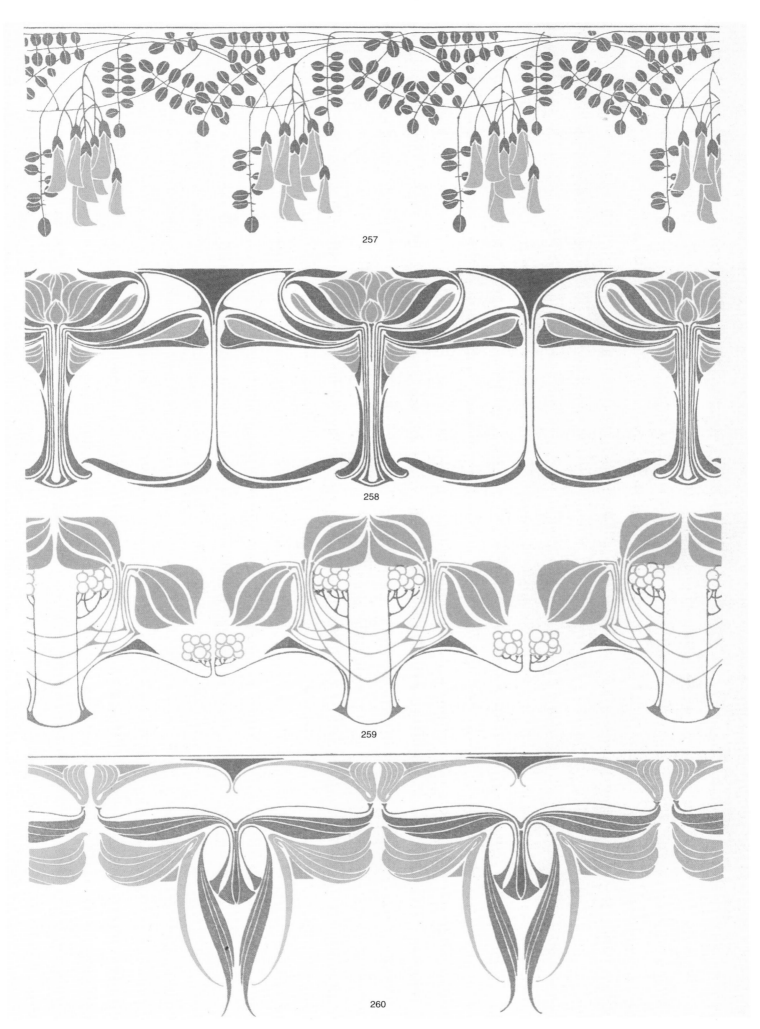

257

258

259

260

R. Beauclair: Wall Friezes

261

262

263

264

265

266

267

268

R. Godron: Floral Ornaments in English Taste

269

270

271

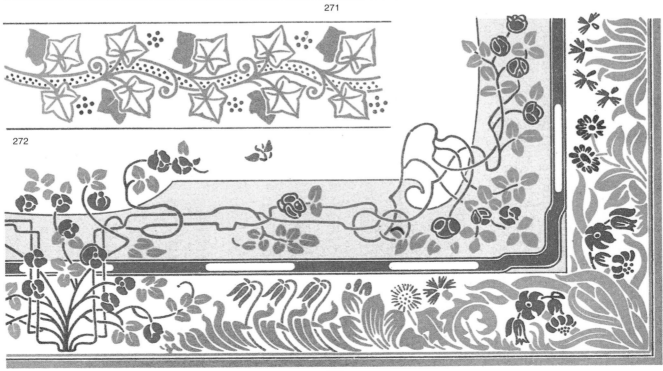

272

273

R. Godron: Modern Borders and Corners

274

275

276

277

278

279

G. Rossmann: Modern Wall Decorations

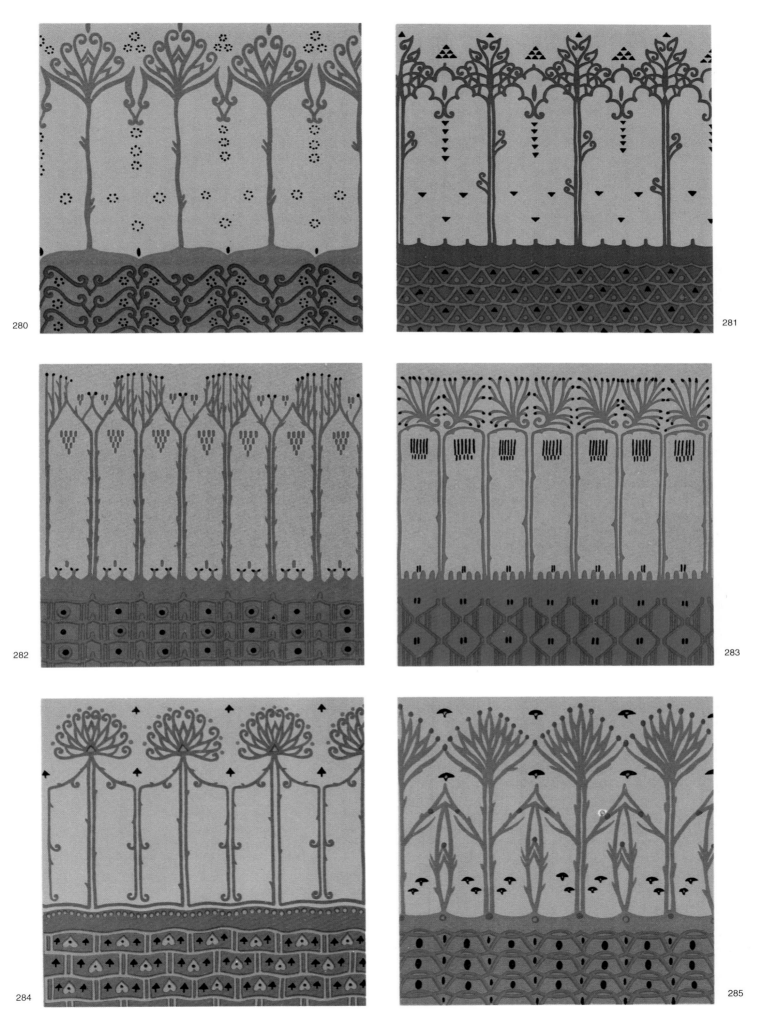

280

281

282

283

284

285

W. Welter: Wall Decorations

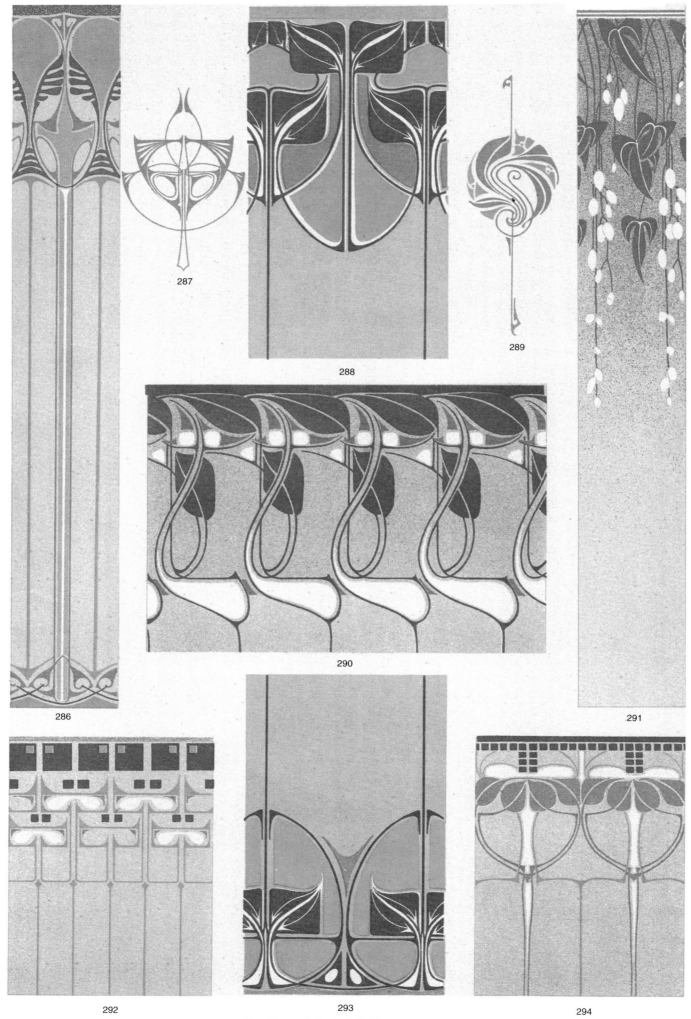

287

289

288

290

286

291

292

293

294

R. Beauclair: Wall Decorations

295

296

297

298

299

300

301

302

M. Dufrène: Modern Ornament

41

303

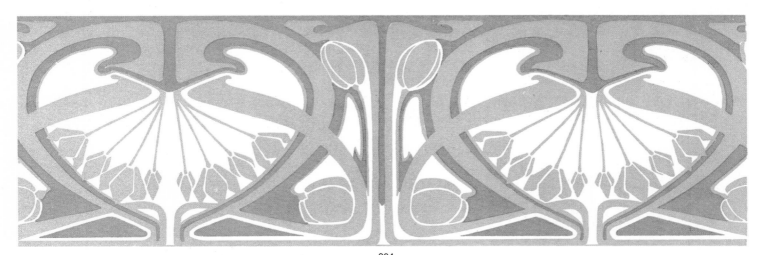

304

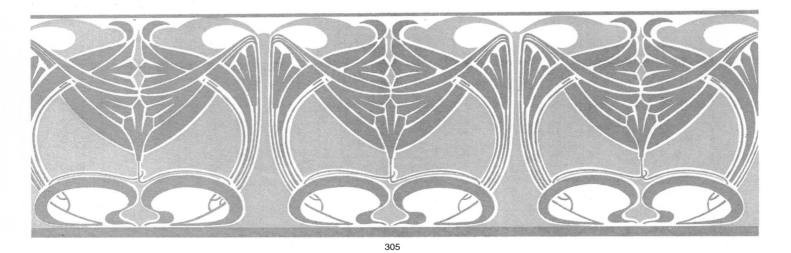

305

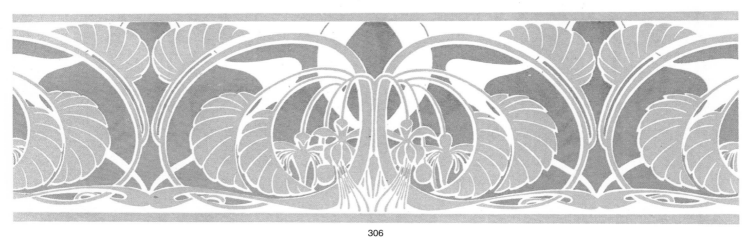

306

A. Petitjean: Modern Borders

307

R. Beauclair: Plates

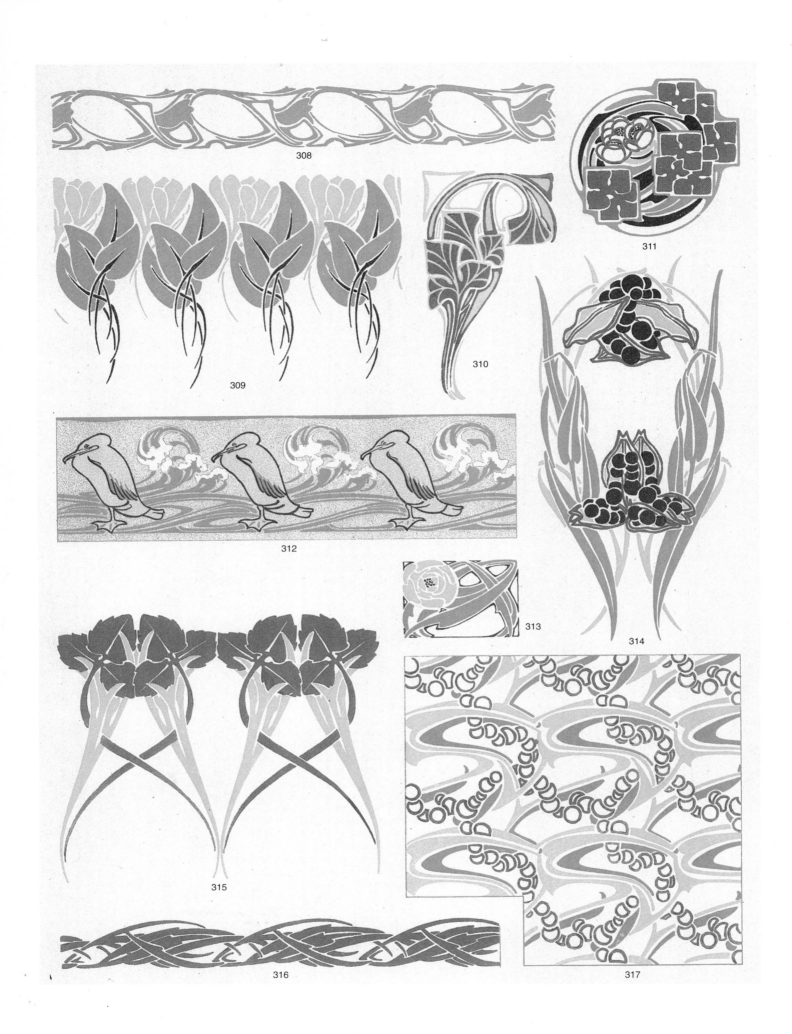

308

309

310

311

312

313

314

315

316

317

M. Dufrène: Friezes and Ornaments